Remember When

a tribute to the vanishing rural landscape

by Mary Rufledt Gladitsch

Mary Rufledt Gladitsch

ISBN 1-930596-06-5

Published by THE GUEST COTTAGE, INC.
P.O. Box 848
Woodruff, WI 54568
1-800-333-8122

Library of Congress Cataloging-in-Publication Data

Gladitsch, Mary Rufledt.
   Remember when : a tribute to the vanishing rural landscape / by Mary Rufledt Gladitsch.
      p. cm.
      ISBN 1-930596-06-5
   1. Farm life--Poetry. 2. Farm life--United States--Pictorial works. 3.
Landscape--United States--Pictorial works. 4. Landscape--Poetry. I. Title.

   PS3607.L33 R46 2001
   811'.6--dc21
                                                            2001040914

Design & Typography by 7C IMAGING

Printed in the United States

CONTENTS

To A Farmer Dying Young (dedication) 1

Moving To The Country 3

Brush Prairie School 5

Horse Power 7

Going Out of Business 9

First Crop 11

Milking Time 13

Barbed Wire Fences 15

Who Wears the Pants? 17

Knowing 19

Corn Shocks 21

Driving Tractor .23

What a Pig! 25

Barn Seen From Highway 53 27

Final Sunset 29

September Song 31

Picking Rock 33

Empty Red Chair 35

Estella 37

August Threshing 39

Ferguson Farm .41

Joe Reiter Homestead 43

LaRose's Store .45

Staring Out The Window 47

Three Square Meals 49

Jaworski Barn 51

Blue and Gold 53

Farm Auction 55

Haymow Visit 57

Fernwood School 59

Trail Farm 61

Weeping Willow .63

Hoarfrost 65

Concrete Fields .67

Remember When 69

Barn Lights at Night 71

Auburn Town Hall 73

Morning Offering 75

The Price You Pay 77

Old Men 79

Vacancy 81

Milk Cans For Sale 83

The Visit 85

Hay Rake 87

Hungry Run Barn 89

Tillinghast 91

Rootbeer Stand .93

Green Fishing Boat 95

Carlson School .97

Winter's Still 99

Goodwill Offering 101

Noble School 103

White on White 105

Let's Wait 'Til Spring 106

Acknowledgments 107

To A Farmer Dying Young

That look upon his face
is etched within my heart
Honest, Open, Real
Approving from the start
He never had to say
what I know he felt inside
The farming life
His kids and wife
A source of endless pride
The apple of his eye
was me
His only little girl
To see that look upon his face
for that
I'd give the world

This book is dedicated to
my Dad, Ted (Sonny) Rufledt Jr.
(1918-1984)

Moving To The Country

City living has its place.
Some would never trade
the asphalt jungle pressing in
for gardens and a spade.

But those who seek a different path
in search of calmer ground,
do not go back,
no longer lack
the gentle peace they've found.

Endless fields of clover,
doors now open wide,
invite the soul to settle in
take comfort, step inside.

A sanctuary welcoming
where simple living thrives.
A piece of land to call your own
a dream has come alive.

◀ Lueck Farm
now owned by
Mike & Patti Rufledt

Tom & Catherine
Rubenzer, 1854 ▶

3

Brush Prairie School

I have fallen in love
with a one room school
A romantic diversion
which knows no rules

My mind can create
a well preserved past
Beautiful memories
an image that lasts

Of days when the young
would learn from the old
Of times when a book
was a pleasure to hold

A romantic excursion?
Think I'm a fool?

I have fallen in love
with a one room school

◄ Brush Prairie
School

Classroom inside
Brush Prairie School
circa 1918 ►

Horse Power

The horse was all there was
Working every time
From dawn to dusk
Dependable
Reason for this rhyme

Man and metal
Harnessed power
Living, breathing beast
An engine strong, unfaltering
A partnership now ceased

◀ Hay rake on
rural road
Charlie Hebert
circa 1935 ▶

Haying on Martin
Weber Sr. farm
1937 ▶

7

Going Out of Business

The dime store can't be closing
Please say it isn't so
Main Street America
I hate to see it go

Penny candy, fabric, soap
School supplies come fall
Make up, toys and underwear
Ben Franklin had it all

Why can't some things
Just stay the same
Stand still in time
Yet remain

A penny saved
Early to bed
A penny earned
Ben Franklin's dead

◀ Ben Franklin Store
Dime Store
circa 1943 ▶

9

First Crop

If I could go back
for just one day
To savor the smell
of new mown hay
To ride up high
on bales stacked tall
To see boys in the mow
giving their all

If I could go back
I would take it all in
Timothy
Clover
Alfalfa
and then
At the end of the day
when I crawled into bed
A harvest of sweet dreams
would fill
my head

11

Milking Time

Come boss
Come boss
Cows head for the barn
Steady forever
Life on the farm

Come boss
Come boss
Two times a day
Milking and feeding
Throwing down hay

Come boss
Come boss
Release creamy milk
Another day closer to
sleeping in silk

Come boss
Come boss
Milk prices drop
Stretched to the limit
The farmer
must
stop

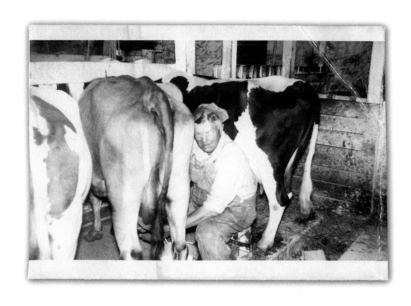

◀ Cow in pasture
Theodore Rufledt Sr.,
my Grandpa,
milking cows
circa 1955 ▶

13

Barbed Wire Fences

Pasture barren
barn now gone
Barbed wire
lingers
on & long

Farmer grows old
farm is sold
Barbed wire
clings
white knuckle hold

Dividing lines
pierce the land
Symbol sharp
simply stands

Outliving its purpose
corpse on display
Barbed wire fence
determined to stay

◄ Barbed wire
fence in winter
Martin Weber Sr.
Farm, 1933 ►

Who Wears the Pants?

Men in the field
Women in the home
Kids doing chores
Roles finely honed

Or so I thought
'til these words came my way
Now I'm not so certain
after what she had to say

If the barn was big
the husband wore the pants
If the house was bigger
he didn't stand a chance

17

Knowing

I knew the day was coming
I saw it from afar
When I would stand here empty
Forgotten, broken barn

I knew my time was over
I watched the farmers go
One by one
Their day was done
This sad farewell
I know

Corn Shocks

Every year
around Halloween
Corn stalks are gathered
In yards they are seen

A fall decoration
A holiday touch
What was once viewed as work
is no longer such
A choice,
not a chore
A pleasure,
an art
A piece of the past
Golden corn
warms the heart

◀ Corn field in
October

Corn shocks
1939 ▶

21

Driving Tractor

The summer
I drove the tractor
was
The summer
I learned what it meant
That summer
was
all about working
That summer
was
meant to be spent
plowing
and
discing
and
putting
up
hay
threshing
and
riding
the
summer
away

◄ Tractor parked
by Carlson School
Ted Rufledt, my Dad,
spreading manure
circa 1957 ►

23

What a Pig!

Ornery
Mean
and
Stubborn
What a fuss you're makin'

You
can
pay
us
back
when
we
turn
you
into
bacon!

Barn Seen From Highway 53

Forgotten barn
cradled now by
elderberry bushes
overgrown and
forgotten too

Silent loft
echoing with
young boys' sweat

Sweet smell of new
mown hay
haunts
your rafters

Harvest memory
grows
dim

◄ Joe Walsberger
farm

Chickens on Joe
Walsberger farm
1934 ►

Final Sunset

Like a soldier you stood
when they burned her
down
Fire, smoke and ashes
fell to the ground

How many summers
did you hold the hay
How many winters
before you turned gray

Did you know they were
planning
the same fate for you
A fiery death
and
your life
would be through

◀ Ray Lane barn

Ray Lane
farmhouse ▶

September Song

Elderberries hanging
purple on the vine
Apples red and ready
ripe harvest time
Yet no one comes to harvest
September's final gift
No urgent need
No mouths to feed
Jars empty
stand clear and stiff
Yesterday the time was now
for filling pantries
filling mows
Today we let it fall and rot
Ungrateful fools
caring not
It makes me sad
to think that I
left it there
to whither and die

◄ Elderberry bush
in September

Apple harvest
circa 1910 ►

Picking Rock

Field stone loaded
on
empty wagons
Kids
walking behind
Bending
Prying
Lifting
Hot, dusty job
Nothing pressing job
No one's favorite job

Rocks
collected
Piled in
ditches
fields
yards
Spent afternoons
clearing fields
of stone

Empty Red Chair

Where have you gone?
When did you leave?
Were you going to come back?
For this do you grieve?

Why did you go?
What led you away?
Were you going to come back
to sit one more day?

Your red chair remains
A reminder to all
We whisper goodbye
with each coming fall

35

Estella

Big room
Little room
Estella Country School
Out on Highway E
Children learned the rules

Big kids
Little kids
lined up in a row
Memorizing facts
Did they ever know

Big dreams
Little dreams
waiting to awake
Outside the brick
and mortar
A larger step to take

◀ Estella Country
School
Estella class picture
circa 1959 ▶

August Threshing

When the oats turned golden
and the weather was just right
it was time to cut and harvest
in bundles round and tight

Shocks standing tall and ready
pale ochre, blonde and dried
Bundle teams of men and boys
prowess to be tried

Threshing machine entered the scene
designed to lick the chore
Inhaling crops from fields of gold
filled, yet wanting more

Conveyor in front
pulled in grain like a jaw
While a beater would strip
the oats from the straw

A crew of ten or twenty
worked long with little rest
Neighbors helping neighbors
Teamwork at its best

◀ Threshing machine
Threshing crew
circa 1934 ▶

Ferguson Farm

Stone creation
work of art
Sandstone sets
this barn apart
Sturdy structure
red and tan
Cook's Valley Quarry
graces the land
Stone upon stone
layers of sand
grain upon grain
Foundation grand

◄ Emil & Annie
Raatz farm
later owned by
Gordy Ferguson

Martin Weber
working on stone
foundation
1939 ►

41

Joe Reiter Homestead

Our house will be large
Impressive estate
Perched on a hill
Seymour view great

With room to grow
We'll build it strong
Holding family close
Life will be long

Now spirits drift
Through windows broken
Empty rooms whisper
Hopes once spoken

◄ Reiter homestead
Joe Reiter family
circa 1890 ►

LaRose's Store

Up north by my cabin
there is a corner store.
It's never been remodeled;
they seldom scrub the floor.
Canned goods stand stiff and dusty.
The cheese just might have mold.
But this is where I love to shop;
on me, it has its hold.
Campbell's soup that once was red
is now a faded blue.
The expiration date could be from 1992.
Kids have always worked there.
Grandma Edna bakes the bread.
Bobby fills the goody jar
with nuts and bolts and thread.
Gas, booze, leaches,
plumbing parts, and more,
you'll find the local talent
posted by the door.
I've never seen the basement,
but it's been described to me
as an endless maze of cubby holes
filled with junk from A to Z.

I love this store, I cannot bear
that now it has been sold.
The last remaining general store,
its story must be told.
I hope they never change a thing
or clean out any corner.
For if they do, I'll wear black
and become LaRose's Mourner.

◄ LaRose's store
LaRose's
circa 1960 ►

Staring Out The Window

Vine, green and growing
settled on the sill
Window tall and knowing
Silent
Open
Still
Every gaze once gathered
long aching stares
Now released
through open pane
Free
without care

◄ Maplewood
School window

Maplewood
School ►

Three Square Meals

Three times a day
we gathered 'round
Each in our place
a belonging we found
Bacon and eggs
Pancakes from scratch
Hot fresh bread
Rhubarb jam, a new batch

It was one thing to count on
solid as stone
The family and food
no going alone
Milk from the barn
Corn from the field
Home grown veggies
Summer garden, our meal

Mom canned for the winter
Dad hunted the deer
We lived off the land
from year to year

◄ Ted & Toni Rufledt
farm house
Rufledt Christmas
dinner, 1968 ►

49

Jaworski Barn

This barn has a story
was all she had to say.
Stanley and Raynelda
have the whole history.
So I dialed up their number
and gave them a call.
What a tale was in store
from that barn standing tall.
It was built in the '20s
on 80 acres of land.
Building a house was
part of the plan.
Spring brought change
with more acreage to buy.
Good land and a house,
on Highway M it did lie.
Moving the barn
with a horse team of two
seemed a daunting task,
yet one they would do.
The horses were hitched.
That barn was then hauled
on logs tied together
until they were stalled.

Stuck on the highway
for most of the day;
digging a trench
so the anchor would stay.
Finally at dusk
the move was complete.
It stands proud today,
a remarkable feat.

◄ Stanley & Raynelda
Jaworski farm
Brunos Jaworski barn
1946 ►

Blue and Gold

Corn and foxtails
stand brilliant
against
cobalt blue
skies

One of the last
warm
sweet
days of autumn

No bluer blue
Nor truer gold
Will artist's palette
ever hold

◄ Field on AA
Grain at Martin
Weber Sr. farm
1939 ►

53

Farm Auction

Who will give me five?
Do I hear ten?
Going once
Going twice
Auctioneer calls again

Buckets of nails
Pitchfork and pails
Blood, sweat and tears
Farmer's life for sale

Off to new owners
No more to belong
Going once
Going twice
Going
Going
Gone

Haymow Visit

I saw the light
and it was you
checking in on me
Spirit drawn
from up above
I sat down on your knee

You told me all the crops
were in
The price of milk was high
You and Mom
had just sat down
to homemade apple pie

I saw the light
and cried your name
and begged for you to stay
With a hitch in your step
you turned
toward the field
and
slowly walked away

◀ Haymow on
Rufledt farm

Tom, Mary, Ted &
Mike Rufledt
1956 ▶

Fernwood School

Close the door
Bus them into town
Efficiency in numbers
Like age gathered 'round

Close the door
Throw away the key
Lock up this one room building
we called community

Close the door
Say your last farewell
What was lost
when the doors were closed

Time
will only tell

◄ Fernwood
schoolhouse
Fernwood School
circa 1965 ►

59

Trail Farm

If you go to Trail Farm
to ski the miles of snow
Take the outer loop
with silo
bronze and gold
A monument from 1912
A one time working farm
where Downey sent
his wife and boys
to keep them safe from
harm
A tree grows through the
middle
as if to tell us all
Relax
Go ski
Have some fun

Like me
Your days will soon be
done

Weeping Willow

I weep for you willow
a silent tear
of days gone by
a memory dear

Cradled dreams
once held in your arms
Now drift on the wind
now rain
on my farm

Hoarfrost

Hoarfrost
Hanging heavy
Icy apparition
Crystal filigree
Stand and stare
Linger there
Diamonds sparkle bright
Stop and gaze
on
Calm clear days

Hoarfrost
Winter white

◀ Gladitsch barn
Richard Rufledt
circa 1950 ▶

Concrete Fields

You who were here before me
are you listening to me now?

Did the fields you tilled
with your horse drawn plow
turn out the way
you had hoped somehow
or has the course of time
turned your dreams into concrete
screaming for relief

The buildings and cars
and the stores and the bars
are crowding the deer in the field
And the house that you built
for your wife and your kids
is now covered
with blacktop and steel

We keep moving ahead
and do anything
to keep from looking back
Afraid we might see
what we know wasn't meant to be

With only us to blame
we all stand in shame and ask
where has it all gone?

Remember When

Remember when the days were long
A life could just unfold
Seasons planned the jobs at hand
Each harvest edged in gold

Remember when the crib was full
Corn for hungry cows
Holsteins grazed in every field
Hay in every mow

Remember when we all sat down
To three big meals a day
Homegrown food, unhurried talk
Heads bowed, a time to pray

Remember when much less was more
When we were not alone
A real person answered
When you called them on the phone

Remember when a single room
Could function as a school
One teacher meeting all the needs
Kids learned the Golden Rule

Remember when the farming life
Slowly slipped away
Each building a reminder
Shrines to yesterday

◀ Corn Crib in fall
Mary & Jim Rufledt
on family farm
winter 1962 ▶

Barn Lights at Night

Lights on in the barn
still make me smile
Knowing someone is home
I go back for a while

What a treasure I had
as a kid on the farm
returning at night
to that glow shining warm

Day after day
Night after night
Secure I could count on
my dad
and those lights

◀ Ted Rufledt farm
Rufledt farm
circa 1950 ▶

71

Auburn Town Hall

Through nettles, trees and tangled vine
I made a path to look inside
And there still standing pale blue
A stage where child actors grew
Children reciting rhymes & poems
Dickinson, Frost, Emerson, Holmes
Paul Revere's Ride, Longfellow's plea
Yeats and Lake Isle of Innisfree
Memorable words from authors now past
Return and remind
The written word lasts

◄ Auburn Town Hall
Charlie Wenzel
circa 1919 ►

Morning Offering

Dawn breaks
like a silent prayer.
Who can find
fault
with this day.

Dawn breaks
like a precious gift.
Open it gently
and pray.

◄ John J. Hassemer
family farm

Viola Hassemer Grill
& Harold Hassemer
summer 1961►

Wallace Hassemer
circa 1935 ►

The Price You Pay

One lost a finger
One lost an arm
Another his life
while working the farm
Big enough
to reach the pedals
Old enough
to drive
Chores to be done
Pride to be won
The trick was staying alive
On the job training
OSHA had no say
Man and boy worked
side by side
Beware
The price you pay

◀ Tom & Jan
Rufledt farm
Steve Rufledt
circa 1945 ▶

Old Men

Old men know what work is
Wide hard hands of steel
Old men know their women
Praise at every meal
Old men know the weather
Nature reigns supreme
Old men know an honest life
What's said is what they mean
Old men are unflappable
They cannot be deterred
Old men are deliberate
Purpose they prefer
Venerable
Honorable
Genuine
True
Trustworthy
Wise
Old Men Rule

◄ Tom Lewis
Round Lake
E.R. Ballard
Frank Dutton
Ed Kranzfelder
Homer Emmerton
Fred Dutton
William Bauer
1905 ►

79

Vacancy

◀ Henry Wendt farm
now owned by
Tony Hillebrand

William Rogge &
son, Jerome
circa 1920 ▶

Hornets make a home
under shaded eve
Hollow shell house
invites me in
draws me close
Shadow children
spill out of
yesterday's door
Abandoned milk cans
wait and wait
and
wonder
When will they be back

Milk Cans For Sale

You stood before the firing squad
rusted, worn and proud
Two lifetimes of hauling milk
etched upon your brow
Hoisted once by callused hands
backs and arms your slave
All salute before
they shoot
and
send you to your grave

◄ Milk cans at
Rufledt auction

Armour & Company
Milk condensery
circa 1920 ►

The Visit

People used to visit
An hour would slip by
Talks about the crop of corn
Time in rich supply

People used to drop in
Then stay for half the day
Each filling up the other
with all they had to say

People used to visit
Their purpose plainly known
To simply share their daily life
and feel less alone

Was there more time
a few years back
Do we no longer need
The luxury of a visit
Our precious minutes bleed

◄ Forrest Whipple's
home

Eli & Delvina,
Mary & Jake
playing cards
circa 1935 ►

Hay Rake

Forrest took one look
and claimed it as his own
Red and rusted
skeleton
standing all alone

Forrest took one look
and saw his younger days
Helping friends and neighbors
harvest bales of hay

Forrest took one look
and knew it as his last
Days of raking hay
live on
only
in his past

◀ Forrest Whipple's
hay rake

Richard Rufledt
raking hay
circa 1950 ▶

Hungry Run Barn

◀ John Burnell farm
now owned by
Robert Tenley

Biddy & Rex
Horse team owned
by William Rogge
circa 1920 ▶

The worse use a barn can get
is no use
none at all
Years of hollow days and nights
invite the coming fall

Beams to boost
a sagging back
Aging
aching bones
Fresh coat of paint
on faded boards
Spectrum long outgrown

Hats off to those
who breathe new life
whose efforts now revive
Picture perfect
Artist's dream
Currier and Ives

Tillinghast

◀ Tillinghast School
Mile Corner School
Judy Raven
Sharon Oldenberg
Donna Ziebell
Tommy Richards
Paul Channing
David Boese
Raymond Flint
Judy Pederson
circa 1955 ▶

A former student spoke to me
Words so soft and kind
Velvet memories cushion the past
Soothe the present mind

Do we remember only the good
The comforting times of then
Do we remember
and choose to forget
The struggle of life
back when

Rootbeer Stand

On a hot summer day
There's no finer way
To soothe the fiery season
Than to stop for a while
And catch the smile
Of a car hop aimed for pleasin'
Frosty mugs of rootbeer
Milky white cones of cream
Once a family favorite
Now
Just a dream

◄ Mary Ann's
Rootbeer & More

Bresina Tire and
Rootbeer Stand
1937 ►

Green Fishing Boat

SEP · 67 ·

◄ Fishing boat
in swamp
Breezy Point Road

Joe & Diane Poirier
1967 ▶

It was just another day
when you left me here
Leaves wearing gold
in the fall of the year
Certain to return
one warm spring day
Yet still I wait
So still I stay
Seasons come and seasons go
Forgotten dreams
of these I know

Carlson School

Runny leaded windows
Cedar shingles rotten
Gray on gray
So much to say
A building long forgotten
Reading 'Riting 'Rithmetic
Gathering wood for heat
Travel back and forth to school
Depended on your feet

◀ Carlson School
Mile Corner School
circa 1955 ▶

Winter's Still

Shorter days of winter
Evening comes at five
Stew is on the stove
Family pulled inside

Darkness stops the flurry
Hurried pace of day
Wood stove flickers warm
Melting shades of gray

Frost arrives in white lace
on the window sill
Feet enclosed in woolen socks
escape the drafty chill

Close to home
all gathered near
Welcome
Winter's Still
is here

◄ Dan & Kathy
Faschingbauer barn
Dennis Poirier
1967 ►

Goodwill Offering

History is recorded
in those staves stacked high.
All that remains
to tell the tale
of love
when someone dies.
Every farmer and family too
turned out that hot June day,
to ease the troubled
bedridden mind
and
bale the new mown hay.
Women put on aprons,
baked bread and cooked the food.
Men divided up the job,
each given work to do.
When that day
came to an end,
silent silo knew,
A dying man was not alone,
his neighbors
all came through.

◄ Emory & Wilma
Anthony silo

Henry Hanson and
James Seibel haying
1938 ►

Nobel School

One thing they'll remember
When all is said and done
A teacher who was not afraid
To let them have some fun

Spring brought chores for children
Combining work and play
Raking up the grassy lawn
Those final days of May

A fire for burning twigs and leaves
Roasting marshmallows sweet
A teacher to warm the hearts of all
Who gathered for this treat

One thing they'll remember
When school is faded gray
A teacher who was not afraid
To trust and seize the day!

◀ Nobel School
End of year
clean up and
marshmallow roast
at Nobel School ▶

Elton Kelm
Sylvan Zwiefelhofer
Robert Dallman
Richard Kressin
Robert Zwiefelhofer
Duane Boettcher
circa 1958 ▶

White on White

I always like a red barn
standing stark
against the snow
I always like some contrast
comparing
what I know
But when I saw
white on white
simple
plain
pure
I felt a beauty
quietly soft
Monotone
Allure

Raymond & Juverna
Hilson farm
January road
1940 ▶

Let's Wait 'Til Spring

by My Mother, Toni Reiter Rufledt

"Let's wait 'til spring to sell the farm," said he.
"OK" said I, "it's all right with me."
Then spring rolls around and the fields are green.
And the plow and planters appear on the scene.
It rains the wrong times and the weather's too hot.
Three cows die and two have hoof rot.
Insects find their way to the corn.
He gets stuck on the tractor
and his pants get torn.
First it's too wet and then it's too dry.
He's behind in his schedule and he wants to cry.
He can't get a combine when he should.
He'd buy his own if he only could.
Along about November the harvesting's through.
Mows, silos, bins are full;
there's not much to do.
"Let's wait 'til spring to sell the farm," said he.
"OK" said I, "sounds great to me."
"This is the only life for me," said he.
Rocking and resting so comfortably.
There are drifts of snow outside the door.
But the wood stove takes care of the chill once more.
I look at him and once again feel
a sense of pride for over thirty-four years
of sharing his happiness, hardships and tears.

Said he, "We've had our share of troubles, it's true,
but if we could change our lifestyle, what would we do?"
He has some pain in his chest these days
and wonders if milking those cows really pays.
But he takes a rest 'til it goes away
and usually works a very long day.
Someday he won't farm, but not quite yet.
It might be the day we get out of debt.
"Let's wait 'til spring to sell the farm," said he.
"OK" said I, "whatever will be will be."

*My father died the following summer
after a long day of haying*

Acknowledgments

I wish to thank my husband, Dick, and my two sons, Michael and Carl, for their constant support and encouragement; Tim Callies, for his talent in graphic design; Elaine Gladitsch, for always being there; Teri Gladitsch Mills, for motivating me to take pictures; Melinda Sonquist Gladitsch, for her inspiration and guidance. A special thanks to my brothers, Tom, Mike, & Jim, for their part in creating fond memories of life on the farm. And finally, a heartfelt thank you to family, friends and new acquaintances who helped in honoring the rural past.

pg. 3 . . . . . Tom & Catherine Rubenzer - property of Willard Rogge
pg. 5 . . . . . Classroom in Brush Prairie School - property of Steve Rufledt
pg. 7 . . . . . top: Charlie Hebert - property of Mary Gladitsch
         bottom: Haying on Martin Weber Sr. Farm †
pg. 9 . . . . . Ben Franklin Store, Bloomer, WI †
pg. 11 . . . . Haying days - property of Bill & Judy Hable Family
pg. 13 . . . . Ted Rufledt Sr. milking by hand - property of Mary Gladitsch
pg. 15 . . . . Barbed wire fences †
pg. 17 . . . . Valentine Miller family - property of Donna Bourget
pg. 19 . . . . Bertram Seibel spring harrowing †
pg. 21 . . . . Corn on Martin Weber Sr. farm †
pg. 23 . . . . Ted Rufledt spreading manure - property of Mary Gladitsch
pg. 25 . . . . Slaughtered hog at Martin Weber Sr. farm †
pg. 27 . . . . Chickens on Joe Walsberger farm †
pg. 29 . . . . Ray Lane farmhouse - photograph by Michelle Richter
pg. 31 . . . . Picking apples - property of Bloomer Historical House
pg. 33 . . . . Field stone †
pg. 35 . . . . Mayme Bernier & friends - property of Mary Gladitsch
pg. 37 . . . . Last day of school at Estella - property of Mary Gladitsch
pg. 39 . . . . Threshing machine & crew †
pg. 41 . . . . Foundation at Martin Weber residence †
pg. 43 . . . . Reiter family - property of Mary Gladitsch
pg. 45 . . . . LaRose's Store - property of Edna LaRose
pg. 47 . . . . Maplewood School - property of Mary Gladitsch
pg. 49 . . . . Rufledt family gathering - property of Mary Gladitsch
pg. 51 . . . . Jaworski barn - property of Stanley & Raynelda Jaworski
pg. 53 . . . . Grain at Martin Weber Sr. farm †
pg. 55 . . . . Deb Knight's auction †
pg. 57 . . . . Ted Rufledt and family - property of Mary Gladitsch
pg. 59 . . . . Fernwood School - property of Ione Cole
pg. 61 . . . . Steve Rufledt - property of Steve Rufledt
pg. 63 . . . . Willow on Rufledt farm - property of Mary Gladitsch
pg. 65 . . . . Hoarfrost - property of Steve Rufledt
pg. 67 . . . . Plowing on William Albrect farm †
pg. 69 . . . . Mary Gladitsch & Jim Rufledt - property of Mary Gladitsch
pg. 71 . . . . Ted Rufledt farm - property of Mary Gladitsch
pg. 73 . . . . Charlie Wenzel - property of Elaine Gladitsch
pg. 75 . . . . left: Viola Hassemer Grill & Harold Hassemer
         right: Wallace Hassemer - property of Wallace Hassemer

pg. 77 . . . . Steve Rufledt on tractor - property of Steve Rufledt
pg. 79 . . . . Round Lake lunch - property of Bloomer Historical House
pg. 81 . . . . Man & child with horses - property of Willard Rogge
pg. 83 . . . . Armour's Condensery, Bloomer - property of Norbert Ruff
pg. 85 . . . . Eli, Delvina, Mary & Jake - property of Mary Gladitsch
pg. 87 . . . . Raking hay - property of Steve Rufledt
pg. 89 . . . . Child with horses and sled - property of Willard Rogge
pg. 91 . . . . Children at Mile Corner School - property of Verna Klemish
pg. 93 . . . . Bresina Tire & Rootbeer Stand †
pg. 95 . . . . Poirier kids on Bloomer Pond - property of Roberta Poirier
pg. 97 . . . . Children in classroom - property of Verna Klemish
pg. 99 . . . . Dennis Poirier - property of Roberta Poirier
pg. 101 . . . Haying on Martin Weber Sr. farm †
pg. 103 . . . Last day of the year at Nobel School - property of Verna Klemish
pg. 105 . . . Road west of Martin Weber Sr. farm †
pg. 106 . . . Ted & Toni Rufledt - property of Mary Gladitsch

All present day photography by Mary Rufledt Gladitsch except the following:
Teri Gladitsch Mills, Cover photo, pgs. 6, 12, 24, 66, 76;
Mike Rufledt, pg. 2; Donna Bourget, pg. 16; Kathy Faschingbauer, pg. 98

† photographs by Martin Weber

Martin Weber (1886-1978)
Martin Weber was a carpenter, farm hand, logger and photographer who lived in Bloomer, Wisconsin for most of his life. His collection of photographs is now owned by Norbert Ruff.